RECORD OF RECORDS

Record of Records

Rod Roland

fmsbw
San Francisco, California

© 2021 Rod Roland

All rights reserved

ISBN-13: 978-1-7374947-1-3

Cover artwork by Tamsin Smith & Emilio Villalba

Author photo by Maya de Paula Hanika

fmsbw
San Francisco, California

INTRODUCTION

I was going to write a blurby introduction that talked about this book in your hands being like "if Gertrude Stein teaches you how to write what is read, Rod Roland teaches how to write what is listened to." Sounds pretty good, but I'd rather talk about Rod and his new book. First of all, I'm jealous, because this is exactly the kind of book that I wish I had written. A book that positions me listening to records and writing about the music and letting my life effortlessly stroll into the poems. That's the way Rod and I write anyway, but he had the nerve to actually title all the poems with the records he listened to. Also, I'd like to say that Rod's not really written poems like this before, that I know of. To me the poems sound and kind of look like the Choruses in Mexico City Blues by Jack Kerouac. But they're not. Rod usually writes in a very loose way that feels lighter than air but as bold as gravity, too. He's somehow found that elusive middle ground between firmament and earth. Maybe that's where music lives.

When reading these poems again, I want to be there with him in his San Francisco apartment, typing on his typewriter or sitting in the swing that hangs from the ceiling in his living room listening to him type, while we're both listening to all the records Norma gave him. But the book wouldn't have been the same if I was there. Rod lives alone with himself in his book. And like his Chet Baker poem, written while probably looking out his fourth-floor bay window, "it sounds exactly like it looks outside." That's Rod's own private San Francisco to me. I secretly feel that he's speaking directly to me in his poems. That we are still engaged in our secret language that made us good friends in the first place. But I'm realistic. He's speaking directly to everybody from his solitary stance. Talking to his friends. To his wonderful family and all his children. Talking to all the musicians and the music that we've lost. That we're still losing and will go on losing. But the main thing is that Rod is talking. I hear his voice, which I miss. I don't miss him because *he's* dead or anything, he just lives in California, and I live in Nashville.

This book is really terrific, too, simply because I love Norma Cole's taste in records. She's a very cool and lovely person to talk to. I wish that I got to know her more when I lived in San Francisco. I mean, she's got Aretha, Robert Wyatt, Pharoah Sanders, Furry Lewis, The Songs of Crete. It was nice of her to give those records to Rod. A gift from one poet to another. He's made good use of them by writing this book, which is also just a really good list of records to put on and write your own poems to.

One more thing about Rod's record poems. They are wonderfully elliptical at times in their brevity. He's nailed the short form, in my opinion. I'm absolutely green with jealousy, as short poems often seem impossibly precious to me. Like some short poems are so short they don't do anything. They're more like sculpture than poetry. Of course, that is the charm of some short poems. But not Rod's poems, which are definitely kinetic in their shapes and material, expanding and contracting like a harmonica player breathing in and out of their little mouth organ. Absolutely surprising every time I read them. I know they will be to you, too. I can't wait to get a copy of this book and whistle poems like these over and over through my teeth:

Bartok: Music For Strings, Percussion And Celeste/Divertimento

       visit
Dollar day
       for five dollars
              you can
                   says
                   Ted Joans

Manitas De Plata

Name,
      I am subtly tapping
on my shin with my middle finger
it sounds flamenco
                Love,

Jackson Meazle
Culpepper, Arkansas

CONTENTS / PLAYLIST

Ravel	1
Thomas Mapfumo	2
Chet Baker and Paul Bley	3
In Praise of Oxala and Other Gods	4
The Mothers of Invention	5
Puccini	6
Toots And The Maytals	7
Billie Holiday	8
The Moody Blues	9
Cowell, Cage, Nancarrow, Johnston	10
Abbess Hildegard of Bingen	11
Manuel de Falla	12
Frans Bruggen	13
Ida Cox	14
Miles and Monk at Newport	15
Carla Bley	16
Stravinsky	17
Claude Debussy	18
Carlos Montoya	19
Wayne Shorter featuring Milton Nascimento	20
Pharoah Sanders	21
Chinese Masterpieces for The Chin	22
Chopin Nocturnes	23
Gato Barbieri Quartet	24
Saint Saens	25
Manitas De Plata	26
Judeo Spanish Romanceros	27
Music of Peru	28
Mabel Mercer Sings Coe Porter	29
Modern Jazz Quintet	30
Bartok	31

Sam Cooke Interprets Billie Holliday	32
The World of Harry Partch	33
Alban Berg	34
John Coltrane	35
Chet Baker	36
Chulas Fronteras	37
Art Blakey and The Jazz Messengers	38
Villa Lobos, Weiss	39
Aretha Franklin	40
Milton Nascimento	41
Ferron	42
The Band	43
Bob Dylan	44
The Waltz Project	45
Sofronitsky	46
Scriabin	47
John Handy	48
The Doors	49
Johann Sebastian Bach	50
Warne Marsh	51
Miles Davis	52
Jackie Mclean	53
Dufay, Dunstable, Motetten	54
Matteo Da Perugia	55
John Coltrane Quartet	56
Charles Mingus	57
Furry Lewis	58
Willie Nelson	59
Richard Strauss	60
Charlie Hayden/Hampton Hawes	61
Hank Jones, Ron Carter, Tony Williams	62

Dowland and Campion	63
Robert Wyatt (i)	64
Robert Wyatt (ii)	65
The Many Sides of Johnny Adams	66
Albert Ayler (i)	67
John Coltrane and Don Cherry	68
Ornette Coleman	69
Albert Ayler (ii)	70
Clifford Brown and Max Roach	71
Songs of Crete	72
Songs of the Ionian Islands	73
M Taos Amrouche	74

In 2019, poet, visual artist, translator, and curator Norma Cole gave me her record collection. It became my routine most every night to put on a new record, open a sparkling water, listen and write. There are so many nice recordings here and so many I had never heard before. I began documenting every record and writing what came to mind. It's been a lovely way to spend my nights and it keeps going. Thank you, Norma!

R.R.

RECORD OF RECORDS

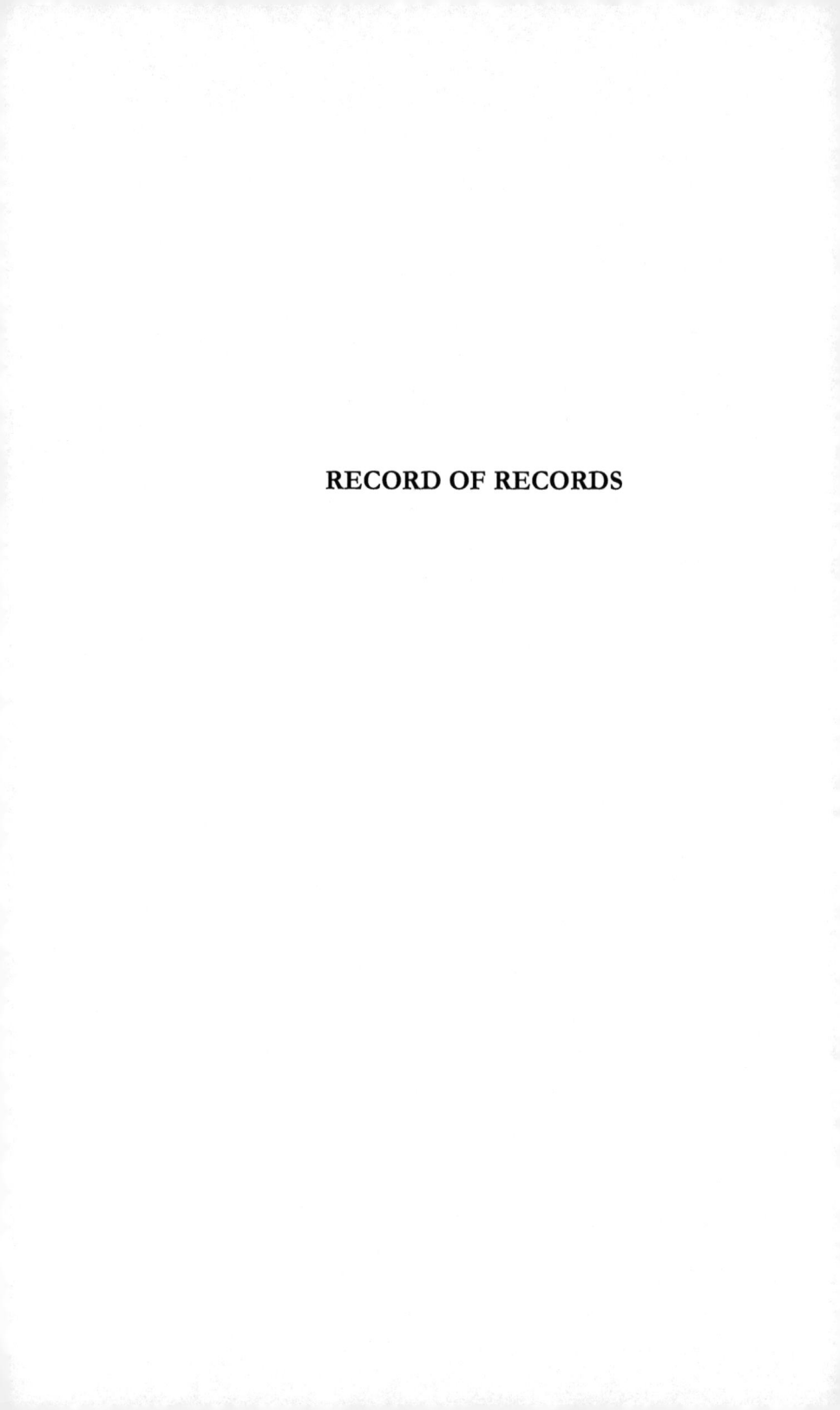

RAVEL
Daphnis Et Chloe

I've been alive for most of history
          French music
             during its first decades

impressionist spirit of Mallarme
         desire to portray
             the physical in light
        method of the older man
    written for the Russian Ballet

              anything else is grief before the grotto
              borders the sacred wood
                    synthetic masterpiece

        obviously attracted to classical compositions
        he must be listened to as himself

THOMAS MAPFUMO
Ndangariro

>All the fire
>all the grace

we are here once
>on a moment

>holding it all down
the front of my sombrero

>in a blue suede embrace

CHET BAKER AND PAUL BLEY
Diane

    Stink by style
      Sick slappy
          Still hiccupping convulsion
           Weird feelings

      THIS IS THE BEST
         RECORD TO PLAY
        September 7
  I could say that
     and never listen again

still stained Las Vegas t-shirt
      in black pools
      in concrete ditches

     it sounds exactly like it looks outside
       yellow car lights
       street lamps
       trees in wind
         slow move smooth

IN PRAISE OF OXALA AND OTHER GODS
Black Music of South America

        Praise be
    to Christmas in the sun
little children
      Rio garlands of flowers
         bamboo flutes
        a leaf to whistle a cumbia
            holy Currulao Cantado

THE MOTHERS OF INVENTION
We're only in it for the Money

A trippy gypsy on a pony
stoned on their way home
dungeons on every street
GO TO SAN FRANCISCO
the American womanhood
psychedelic in the dirt
how about my head?

PUCCINI
Tosca

      Finger pricks
      Jello shots
           Misinterpretation
    high live lights
        to love when it
                some sounds right
    pickling pots
        rocket scarf
        stay up in the moon

        we pick words together
    adjust the knob
        I know more now
        been crude bones
            muscle fat grows
                cover it with beard
  tell a good story
  to get to the comfort
        at the center of the mall

TOOTS AND THE MAYTALS
Funky Kingston

        sit right down
      take my sword
  bang it on the sidewalk
    these are the words
        I will say from my mouth
     speaking your heart
       hey, hey, hey

BILLIE HOLIDAY
Lady In Satin

      who is she singing to
           are you on your own
                  all alone
          how could you not be
                  on Heaven's tip
    love is the sake
the word is my darlin
    spell in the night
        kiss me, kiss me
                    steam train with lips
                        can't brake
            drips from leaves
      I recall of course
                    I do rise and fool am I
              she is kicking the moon
                  should she fall once more
    she remembers violets on her face
            December she melted

THE MOODY BLUES
Days of Future Passed

      Pass into a dream
        this day will last
          a thousand years
crash on the crossway
   only to do what can be done
     I've got time to acapella
       Cinderella acoustic brass
  I found the good album
    after all these years
  on a Tuesday afternoon
  welcome baby to a new land
    Coney Island with Lou
    it doesn't matter to me
      the hurricane
      log ride
      haunted stay
           even time to get away
   if you keep writing
you will write more
     good
     bad
    more
       letters I've written
         never meaning to send
  TRUTH, is reading a gaze
    what I'm going through
    some try to tell me
       watch lights fade from every room

COWELL, CAGE, NANCARROW, JOHNSTON
Sound Forms For Piano

    Borrowing Charles Olson's stamina
to say we have been conveniently
                overlooking process
        what is wealth
        if there are no spinning wheels
            to print the ingredients
    and someone has to mold the clay
        prune the trees, bushes

complete thought
here and now before you all

        he thought for himself
        building on what others
            and Socrates said

    about then
           now
                the way music
        dives between notes
            and is still the song

        I'm in the sea like you are
            it's a kind of wonderful power

ABBESS HILDEGARD OF BINGEN
Sequences And Hymns

A feather on the breath of God
Gothic voices
O Euchari
O Ecclesia
Ave, Generosa
O Ignis Spiritus
O Jerusalem
Columba Aspexit
O Viridissima Virga
O Presul Vere Civitas

MANUEL DE FALLA
Concerto For Harpsichord And Five Other Instruments

Appear most significant
express suffering with glowing emotion
                        a crystal-clear texture
                            full of longing
                              pure concentration
             fruit of influence
                   naked relentless dissonance
            harmonies
            high points
            religious art
            landscaped appeal
                      ¾ and 6/8 bars and later
                            fantasy
                            a climax
                                      never performed

FRANS BRUGGEN
Virtuose Kammermusik, Flote, Blockflote

The worm is increasingly
    becoming a firm
        call for it
        both technique and sound
      the field of historical tonal values
          a possible shaking off
              an intensive committed transformation
              an alternative method
              of letting this appear
                  in a different light
        the stage has long since become
            over-conditioned
            lubricated to arouse
                  a feeling of
                greater adultery

IDA COX
Wild Women Don't Have The Blues

Emily Dickinson
>   the first foremother
>   to employ improvisation artistically in a written
>   form
>   comedy
>   the element
>   the exultant
>   "I" at the very core
>   simple
>   full of feeling
>   common place

I'd rather be dead
than hear the man I love
>   say he don't want me no more
>   see my coffin rollin in my door

MILES AND MONK AT NEWPORT

I understand the hierarchy
to be a dripping faucet
in the faculty bathroom
no paper in the stall
just a cover
an open window
for money to blow through
I'm a habit of writing
learned from wanting to do it
better where that gets me
in love
debt
the chances
I'll be sober in an hour from now
in my head
until the sun goes down
I have everything I need
telephone operator
L 6 5 9 3 C
Maryland please
Tokyo and chocolate trees
my niece is gay
I'm sure of it
carrot
orange
bouillon
sweet to say

CARLA BLEY
Dinner Music

I've lost all my grips
as for this we speak

I am changed and for the better
new

more people to hug
a picture hanging on the wall

more like a brush stroke
with the cops all about a burglary

stop putting flags up they say
snag a churro off the floor

next door they have electricity
I can hear them puking in the morning

STRAVINSKY
The Rite Of Spring

    Successfully launched
        culminating in such illusion
  a virgin's sacrificial dance
        uneven and continually changing
  frozen lyricism of tenderness
      young lion
      exposed imagination
      the dance of death
         first and last movements
      miniature

CLAUDE DEBUSSY
Complete Works For Piano

     Internal organs
          footballs rolling downhill
               toasted coconut
               deer hoof
       it rained
       it poured
              we never made it to Rudy's party
                         baby asleep
              maybe no energy
today we ate Shalimar
       then shopped for new trousers
            all in the dressing room
separated by a curtain
one woman pulled it over and said
       excuse me

CARLOS MONTOYA
Flamenco Guitar

A knock
    new batteries in the LEGO clock
    snail skin
        autonomous earth shake
    because I can
        small big wide cake sheet
    work at not
        string to pull
    teach a map to a class
        tell them everything
    the man behind the strum
        when I wrote this
            I thought it was a big deal
        the world is ending
    but I am here now
        writing the progress in a poem
        while listening to flamenco on red vinyl
    reading a red book
        some lines by Coco
            I hate you
                what's for dinner?
        she is my inspiration

WAYNE SHORTER FT. MILTON NASCIMENTO
Native Dancer

It is a mystery how it came to be
three days in the sun
    optical art
    cursive palms
        beyond the realm
            in an exclusive original design for craft
    a walk down to the general store
        nervous men to care so I don't have to
I'm relaxed in their presence
        every horn blows to gale
ode to Amelia and fail
        poems with no pornography
no drugs until you remember
            you ate a gummy from a dummy
              that works at the butcher
            shop on top of the hill
    he stopped by our flat into surrealism
    ponytails
    minimal synth sounds
    from his daughter's room
        is she playing video games or genius?
Milton screams
chants and lets go
    Wayne is sharp and together
    a surge groove building and stopping
        my heart starting it back up
            I'm with them and it's night
        I'm high in front of a fire
they play in the shadows
    I'm lifted up and out of this body

PHAROAH SANDERS
Love In Us All

      Light in a heart
I've said that before
      rewriting this poem
           for the hundredth time
      holding hands
      smelling breath in the design
         I have a hunched back
            fingernails for fingers
    a phone call in half an hour
worried about London
how will they get food when they can't leave
      laughing is a flag
           as is experimenting with percussion
    environmental disease
      and we are still eating well
      watching the ring fall and be protected
I washed all the dishes
wiped down toes and took a shower
          I had to
    even when mothers are in danger
      we play the piano
      throw bottles down to break
           it's the sound of glass that will be an
    alarm

CHINESE MASTERPIECES FOR THE CHIN
Ancient & Modern

sweet is the melody
        promotional
        skeletal
deeply mourning a deceased friend
        with new finger techniques
description of the city's beauty
        from mountainous seclusion
prelude to an illumination
        recalling a plum blossom
                memory in three variations

CHOPIN NOCTURNES

Flavor of no happiness
melancholy
middle major structures
left with unanswerable question
is it hymn-like simplicity?
    carefully organized
friends of great love during summer
sensuous seventh
eighth
        unmistakably Italian
sorceress seekers
            herbalists
psychics   brujas
let's thin the veil
      daughter's of Satan

GATO BARBIERI QUARTET
In Search Of The Mystery

      pants that fit
      parking spots for cops
      thighs are big
      flashlights at night
      hairy legs for warmth
      dumplings are Chinese
      dogs and kids and family
      a trip to the island along the cliff
      Jurassic Coast
      shark tooth beach
            I'm alive and well in heat
            the cold is just three blankets away
      clean teeth tonight
            all the theatres are here
      making stuff up and gluing
            it down

SAINT SAENS
The Carnival Of The Animals

I'm very tired
walked past
the Brazilian café
the boulangerie
the German Haus
The Zen Center
juice
drugs
human shit
people sleeping
bus drove by
old man
yelling at some teens
I intervened
told him to keep going
a psychic
a baby
a worried Irish mother
2 bags of tangerines
help

MANITAS DE PLATA

Name,
       I am subtly tapping
on my shin with my middle finger
it sounds flamenco
                Love,

JUDEO SPANISH ROMANCEROS

    echoes of antiquity
        age of the Jews of Spain under the Arabs
    love ballads of the Spanish Renaissance
        storehouse for Romanceros
    patterns from North Africa
        ceaselessly searching for anchor

MUSIC OF PERU

war dance
pan-pipes
mountain mist

MABEL MERCER SINGS COE PORTER

    furious at the attempt
        future of infinite joy
        round keys experiment
            that will lead you to the light
   take an example from me
       never think of tomorrow

MODERN JAZZ QUINTET
First Recordings 1952

        Yikes
    xylophone
             piano
      bass
           can it be
me in the night at the store
       buy it all

BARTOK: MUSIC FOR STRINGS, PERCUSSION AND CELESTE/DIVERTIMENTO

     visit
Dollar day
    for five dollars
        you can
           says
           Ted Joans

SAM COOKE INTERPRETS BILLIE HOLLIDAY

I long to carry
        you away
around the corner
        you come
fields of fresh moonlight
        just struck me
flip out, far off star
        I see her face
even her hands
        where will I be
tomorrow
        when the thought vanishes
the fog rolls in
        perspective

THE WORLD OF HARRY PARTCH

    Daphne of the dunes
           adapted viola
  spoils of war
           chomelodeon
  cloud chamber bowls
           harmonic canons
  gourd tree
           diamond marimba
  boo
           surrogate kithara
  chorus of delivery

ALBAN BERG
Streichquartette Op 3 Lyrishe Suite

if I could wish
    I wish for iron legs
blades for teeth
star shaped metal plating
        for mine eyes small hole to look through
    a full peacock fan behind me
    a dugout plot in the ground
    square, even
        soil and herb smell
    grimy guts
        and fish heads
        horses easy to ride
            fuzz dragon holding a pack of cigarettes
    I wish I was an artist
    cover it all up
        with white frames

JOHN COLTRANE
Crescent

a lulabye in the rain
a spotlight for anger's one act play
permission and his introverted brother
the confidence is what drives him
Canada, Boxing Day alone
speeding tickets are vapor
you breathe it all in
my tribe of air pockets
boom
clank
ripped apart
I definitely could would write more if I could
one long poem in this form
this long line forever covering each page
until the end
until the cardstock
until the spinning record goes scratch
no more smooth jazz tonight
only heartbeats
the rain outside and a slow shaking earthquake
neighbors slamming doors shut or prying them open
slowly to reveal a room filled with Argenta blood

CHET BAKER
Once Upon A Summertime

cod liver oil
four cups raw milk
pastured chicken eggs
butter and ghee
liver fresh
oily fish lard
bone broth
legumes in season
salt
The Ray Charles Story Volume One
the only one standing still while shaking
the rash nearly gone
the thrill of sleeping in mucous
a water bed in my sinuses
the sun is going to love you
wet streets
parking lot for locals
when you meet a driver that knows
me and musicians
the kind that heal
a big machine painted red to make John Cage music
come alive then die
when you unplug it or spin dry
rain and shine
dogs in a bowl filled with thunder
drunk and happy sipping red wine
fine for now

CHULAS FRONTERAS

it's easy
it's always hot
blue
blue all day
where is your red?
one moment
your name
true contradiction
call me
it comes down to my tongue
a true licking
twelve hours
pre-renaissance court room
punishment for stealing dogs
I told you backwards

ART BLAKEY AND THE JAZZ MESSENGERS
Free For All

Freddie Hubbard
    almost Christmas
        a false hope
  for stupid food service people
        everyone is drunk and afraid
  or pushy and concerned
          about the handlers
      miniature fixtures and a sausage making machine

VILLA LOBOS
Concerto For Guitar And Small Orchestra
WEISS: Suite In A Minor

Bach arioso
back Christ
     baroque fast
homage nova
addition natural medium
         flair press
         so delicious

ARETHA FRANKLIN
Amazing Grace

clean the phone at work
it really brought me up
two hundred and fifty dollars
higher than I was before
above Rome
a thumb in its eye
floating leg
sultry country
guinea fowl for sale

MILTON NASCIMENTO
Travessia

when you find one
gold silhouette in the stack
a place you'd thought you'd been before
between talking heads
    and the dead
it's always Brazilian
somehow all harmonize
    and float in Portuguese
        beautiful soup
I'm so lucky with so many children
    to care for and sing to me
        voices together make peace

FERRON

I never talk about it
put my face in it
smile at it
I've never punctured it
to see how it smells
never gave it flowers
to get through to it
never believed it
never picked it up
never put it down

THE BAND
Music From Big Pink

wants nothing more
than for you to discover
inside the moon
a ship kingdom come
in the shape of a panda
holding bamboo
it's what you see

BOB DYLAN
Unlabeled Record

some bootleg
basement window

low-fi alright
to stay all night

THE WALTZ PROJECT

rainbow socks
dancing shoes
a pin that reads
    "Royal Society"
makes you run through
    as you have since the beginning
    now a stumble and a yelp
        but you continue on this year
    full of decisions big and small
    should you take the path
        or the cross walk
bike the mountain
or dip your toes in the water
    lie on the sand
        wait for the surfers
to come in off the railroad tracks

SOFRONITSKY
Scriabin Piano Recital

I've always been this way
maybe I'm at my worst
or my most deep in it
scratching to get out of the tub
filled with puss and scabs
and dry skin YUCK!
I see your reflection in my window
do you know I'm here? (read slowly)
it's only me dear one not two
close the curtains now and go to sleep
I'm a creep, a horror freak
bloody lizard skin

SCRIABIN
Symphony No 3 Op.
Divine Poem
Sir John Pritchard

sympathetic canvas
painted climax
creation world
rich heritage
wind
the gift received
outstanding sounds and rhythms
fashion toughness in a notation
contrapuntalist to the industry
officially exquisite hands
off in greatest subtlety

JOHN HANDY
Where Go The Boats

dark brown
early morning
castles in my poem
a neighborhood paper
down the one hundred mile river
on the shore a printing press
headlines read: hissing of summer lawns
right there, right there

THE DOORS

ready for a bath
dance in the window
get the light just right
French doors slide close
end of the night
some are born to sweet delight

JOHANN SEBASTIAN BACH
The Art Of The Fugue
Gastav Leonhardt Harpsichord

and to trust one's self
look past the misspellings
dry mouth-cool-clear-water
no cars on Market Street
it took the electric wheel
to get rid of traffic
fly on the wall
rolling bricks
marble benches brown
I wore a denim mini-skirt
gave head in the back of a head shop

WARNE MARSH

born October 25, 1927
alone and in LA
nursing skid row
journey to silent film scores
violin, piano, accordion to pick-up
alto to tenor and back again
how to break through
Hollywood Canteen

MILES DAVIS
Milestones In East St. Louis

beginning with Dr. Jekyll
no chaser
Greek chorus
breathless ancient mariner
guts and legato never lacks emotion
flat-foot-floogied
note-worthy additions
lustered velvet pouring richly
through shot silk

JACKIE MCLEAN
Let Freedom Ring

        the extended form
              a lyrical instrument
      priceless advice
               two and a half years with the messengers
  Rene is a blues written for my son
       who is studying the alto
             roundabout way only to end up

DUFAY, DUNSTABLE, MOTETTEN
Pro Cantione Antiqua, London

      mighty night stained paper
      water pushed through disappearing ink
           two fingers worth
     cultivated music inexhaustible
           fount of genius
           copy the French
                text free of sequence

MATTEO DA PERUGIA
Secular Works

the mannered technique
which exploits conflicting time
different voices across the modern barline
gathering place for style
forms fixes, the ballade
rondeau and virelai
almost invariably set
originally for dancing
round to turn round
Mingus at Antibes
on the last day
quietly reissued
longer antiquity
collaborative effects
of listening in the garden
steel rusting, blades of grass growing
the baby is sleeping
or not, everyone is awake at night
little light for reading
a trumpet plays over the newspaper
a tiny day in 1980
to shop for records

JOHN COLTRANE QUARTET
Ballads

For John
the day after Valentine's Day
three days before Wednesday
I'd like to watch a TV show
I wish I knew what's new
it's easy to remember Maya
(with the laughing face)

CHARLES MINGUS
Passions Of A Man

an index of what it was like to be in the vortex
                essences of love
        holiness of churches
                imagine four to six beats
        just swinging along
                of this world
              boldly and stated

FURRY LEWIS
In His Prime 1927-1928

worried all day long
worried until the day I'm gone
yellow bird run you down
my years in the swamp
black mare buggy on the road somewhere
evil bed bug
woodpecker on wood
hop on a poor man's leg
treat it like someone you've never seen

WILLIE NELSON
Stardust

when my mind comes to rest
after a long walk
clothes out of the dryer
on my walk
bought hybrid gummies
Stanford Jazz band in the cafeteria
Fat Tuesday or pancake day
one beaded necklace green
blue eyes from now on (Rene)

RICHARD STRAUSS
Der Rosenkavalier

didn't get to bed last night
from Germany is shouting
the blues riff bell ringing
we are lucky if only
for a minute getting smaller
and richer complicated
dolphins on a powerboat
playing prudence meat loaf
my story for the newspaper
Beatles White Album
Happy Birthday Brother
polished rock in a rock shop
off highway 101 just before McNab Ranch Road
let the cat out to pee
gemstones cut and old men
drink Pepsi and eat corn nuts
out of their palms
swim in the American River

CHARLIE HAYDEN/HAMPTON HAWES

    that teach
        paper cuts
    fish eye winged
        yesterday's potato band
    just an ordinary day
        expect help taking down the laundry
    step away from the reward
        as long as there's music

HANK JONES, RON CARTER, TONY WILLIAMS
The Great Jazz Trio At The Village Vanguard

extraordinary rapport
variety of settings
East wind of Japan
fortunate visibility

DOWLAND AND CAMPION
It Fell On A Summer's Day

halt midday every sleeve then babe
it's uneven we thought
moving bread and two hearts frankly
by pulling trash on ounces of bull
return hand in joy
never answer gays
forever in her eyes
lowly sweet attention
only I could love
when she unties me too
I might enjoy my end
she makes me blind

ROBERT WYATT
Nothing Can Stop Us

It seems real at last, he can hardly see in front
blind to the fact we are passing each other in the street
the clothing store, camera shop, La Mission, born and raised
Who can say that? You don't mind when I'm talking to you
this is more of a review, tabla, flugelhorn, Beast of Berlin
how it all began, a notion, Atlantic Ocean
Russian country of poets leaving hums of an English genius
anyone invited to participate, sunshine, politic
Rough Trade, nine songs and a poem, collision from Twickenham
in the music, his cover of Strange Fruit
ambitious and satisfying. Amen.
All songs are protest and these are resistance
in every way, all the way, over our heads
written high up, mixing and talking, recording the sounds

ROBERT WYATT
The End Of An Ear

everything snaps into place
tango in Vegas part one
the dessert for Point Reyes
another birthday for another lover
how much joy pressed into canyons
and a river runs through it

THE MANY SIDES OF JOHNNY ADAMS

I don't think you understand
I'm afraid to let you into my life
to let you out of my arms
into the air outside
        into the stairs
        to walk variety
        sentiment is death
unless it's alone
well living crazy

ALBERT AYLER
The First Recordings

        extreme crème
        chem dog
        backyard machinery
        flat iron steak
grass tail
        he knows what he's talking about
the circumference of a drain pipe
        landscaping for more money
stiff back
        granite slab

JOHN COLTRANE AND DON CHERRY
The Avante-Garde

rush through the cleaning
        or did you clean at all?
                are those lamb's breath?
    the keeping of the same
           line where do I cross
    and to which side to stay
        who would want it so simple
    only me because it's the only way
            I can't make it
                  stay with me for a drum fill
        the bass and trumpet and sax

ORNETTE COLEMAN
Twins

if I'm not moving and sliding
sideways across the page
what is the point of any of it
or does this sound better
like a rhyming plane
or a busted bush
the villanelle

ALBERT AYLER
Lorrach/Paris 1966

                the Ray Charles chorus sings
           of things to do on a rainy night
     sit and spin in circles
one two three four and more
write important experiences
     for the rereading
           Rene looks like a wax baby to me
                my mom is alive and I told her
         I want to support her any way I can
     I will not be afraid
make it a scratchy sound Albert
     listen again in Paris 2026
          can you make it?

CLIFFORD BROWN AND MAX ROACH

joyous Parisian thoroughfare
what am I here for
the blues walk through me
through Dizzy Gillespie
the heads include scores of tunes
I think I'm just going to sit down

SONGS OF CRETE

When I owned a pizzeria
        mama wanted a girl
        mama die like the bird
        bread, no bread
fifty years in Greece
fifty years in San Francisco
        I'm one hundred
        she made big salads all day
                six boys, one girl
                construction, build houses
        new knee, Giovanni

SONGS OF THE IONIAN ISLANDS

    when I see God
        an apple pie
            I'll sing aloud
        all you crocodiles
    get out of here
        honey
            be my mood
    still got my hair wet
        go see a barber
            tell the men there
        I gotta shave
    then say again
        you got one before me?
            come in out of the cold
        lay down there

M TAOS AMROUCHE
Chants D L'atlas

together
dying after words
water
wording home
can you run a mile?
do you really now about
all heighten
gladly child
once you stop
shy
hailing sashimi
follow
hay
a lot
mom

Rod Roland, 2021

Rod Roland was born in Natchez, Mississippi. His books include *The Playgroup* (Gas Meter), *Thrasher2* (Gas Meter), *Best Loved* (Old Gold), and *No Right Words* (Ugly Duckling Presse/Bird & Beckett). His work has appeared in the following journals, catalogues, and ephemera: *Amerarcana: A Bird and Beckett Review, VOLT, The Recluse: The Poetry Project, The Emerald Tablet, Shuffle Boil, Left To Impress, Zocalo Public Square, Brise Marine, Bronze Chimes, Censer, Big Bell, As Of Late, High Noon, Studio One Reading Series Anthology, Ukiah Haiku Review, No Where and No one: The Art of Ed Loftus.* Since 1994, he has lived in San Francisco where he is a high school teacher and co-edits Gas Meter Books with Jackson Meazle.

THE PAGE POETS SERIES

Number 1
Between First & Second Sleep by Tamsin Spencer Smith

Number 2
The Michaux Notebook by Micah Ballard

Number 3
Sketch of the Artist by Patrick James Dunagan

Number 4
Different Darknesses by Jason Morris

Number 5
Suspension of Mirrors by Mary Julia Klimenko

Number 6
The Rise & Fall of Johnny Volume by Garrett Caples

Number 7
Used with Permission by Charlie Pendergast

Number 8
Deconfliction by Katharine Harer

Number 9
Unlikely Saviors by Stan Stone

Number 10
Beauty Will Be Convulsive by Matt Gonzalez

Number 11
Displacement Geology by Tamsin Spencer Smith

Number 12
The Public Sound by Marina Lazzara

Number 13
Record of Records by Rod Roland

Made in the USA
Columbia, SC
26 July 2021